INSTAGRAM MARKETING STRATEGY

Marcos Handley Pixaro

INSTAGRAM MARKETING STRATEGY - 2020

Posting At The Right Time

Timing is everything when using Instagram marketing. Your engagement depends on your timing. If you post at a bad time you might end up being unnoticed. Early morning or late in the evening is the optimal time to post. The worst day for engagement during a week is Sunday while Monday and Thursday tend to possess highest Instagram follower engagement and traffic.

Follow Similar Instagram Profiles

Follow people that follow an equivalent interest you wish . If you follow people with similar interests you will be sure to get noticed. Plus, they are more likely to follow you back. Reach out to people who you believe would be interested in your products.

Get a Suitable Instagram Name

It is unlikely that folks are going to be checking out you by your name unless, you're a star . So create names revolving around your business website or the industry that you simply are working in. Now, when people associated with your industry search the relative keywords, it's more likely that your profile will show up. Here is a powerful Instagram marketing strategy. Make your "user name" just like what you're selling because that's what people are checking out .

Use Description

When writing your description confirm to let people realize the advantages of you and your business. Add a link to your channel or ad campaign to direct the people on your page.

Add Texts To Images And Use Hashtags

Instagram is more better images than plain texts. Adding images may be a good way to let people skills wonderful your product or service is. Use visually strong content that will attract attention.

Everybody needs to use hashtags on Instagram and if you want your business to be noticed then you have use hashtags. Using hashtags will confirm you finish abreast of the list of the trending keywords that folks are checking out .

How Instagram Can Help You To Promote Your Business

When forming your social media strategy for your business, Instagram is a superb mobile marketing app which will effectively carry over your companies marketing strategy. While Instagram is not the only tool that has been proven effective for businesses, it is hard to ignore as it is currently valued at One Billion dollars and 80 million+ users. There are some ways that Instagram are often an enormous benefit when promoting your businesses: marketing strategy, philosophy, and brand image. Here are a few key tips to keeping your Instagram account consistent with your marketing strategy

Create Your Own Unique Hashtag

Creating your own unique hashtag may be a simple thanks to build a loyal following on your businesses Instagram. Once you determine a reputation for your hashtag, confirm that you simply are promoting it to your audience by posting it across all social networks and as a caption on every Instagram post. Instagram also makes it very convenient to watch which followers are actively using your businesses hashtag. I recommend attracting with the users who update your hashtag say him thankful them personally or re-post their photo, and tag them. By recognizing the users who are actively using your hashtag, new users will be encouraged to post as well.

Tagg Your Photos

Tagging your photos on Instagram, will allow your business to involve your community on a completely different level. By tagging photos, your followers will be able to view the location of your business like a: retail store, restaurant, or office location. Tagging is another great way to build your businesses following. If you and a co-worker go out to lunch at Chipotle, you can Tag your photo at the location you are dining at. By doing so, Instagram users who also tag this same location will be able to see your photo, which will hopefully encourage them to follow your businesses account and helping to promote your store and increase revenue for you.

ENCOURAGE EMPLOYEE POST

Some of your most loyal promoters should be your employees. Encourage your employees to be actively involved in posting photos on your businesses account a few times a week. By having your employees on board, users who are following your account will appreciate the ability to get to know more about your company's employees. As long as you set clear guidelines of what is appropriate to post, you should gain a following rather quickly due to the variety of different types of posts your account will consist of.

INSTAGRAM MARKETING STRATEGY

CONNECT YOUR SOCIAL MEDIA ACCOUNTS

Be sure to sync all of your businesses other social media accounts to your Instagram every time you post a photo. Having all of your social media accounts connected, your audience has a high potential to expand, because not all of your fans and followers will follow your other accounts such as: Facebook, Twitter, Tumblr, and Flickr. Syncing up all your other social media accounts not only allows for additional content but an opportunity for more frequent posts.

Why Top Brands Are Using Instagram To Promote Their Business

Basically, Instagram is a mobile-only application (once reserved for iPhone owners, but now also available to Android users) that allows account-holders to take photos of things they like, edit them and upload them to a profile that is visible to their followers. Account-holders can also follow other people's accounts, liking photos that appeal to them and sharing them on through other social networking channels, like Facebook and Twitter. Whilst many may think that the app doesn't have much online marketing value, the top brands of the world have proven otherwise.

Looking at Instagram's statistics, it becomes clear that luxury brands tend to be the most followed by consumers. Brands like Burberry, Tiffany & Co, Armani, Mercedes Benz and Gucci all feature in the top 10 list for the highest amount of followers. These brands were quick to spot a new way in which they could engage consumers through an online marketing campaign that really doesn't feel like one - all they have to do is upload some attractive images of their latest products or lines and let the power of the internet do the rest.

Some brands have really embraced the purpose of Instagram and aren't using the application to promote their latest products and online marketing propaganda at all. Instead, they upload highly attractive (and highly edited) images of their products, taken by professional photographers and fans alike. Whilst the products in some of these images could be a few years old and no longer available brand new, the effect of getting the brand name out there is still the same. This is how Instagram is meant to be used, and followers are quick to recognize this.

In the world's top brands and multinational companies are using Instagram to give their internet marketing business an extra boost, there is a huge opening for some of the more niche brands to get their foot in the door. At the end of the day, it isn't all about the amount of followers you have - the amount of interaction between your followers and images is equally important. Even a brand with a considerably low number of followers (say, a few thousand) could still perform well if user interaction is quite high.

Instagram For eCommerce Marketing

With so many internet business sell their products while competition is at an all time high in the online retail industry. Any eCommerce business wanting to succeed in this competitive environment needs to have the right marketing strategies in place. It's simply not enough to have a great webstore. Without proper marketing all your website development efforts will go down the drain.

There are a few online business marketing strategies you can use to get the best out of your online business success.

1. Upsell Your Products

A majority of merchants go for up selling their products, because up selling works better than cross selling online. There are two main factors to up selling - 1) Make your upsells related to the original products 2) Have the right product pricing strategy to make the upsell look like a deal. Also make sure that products you are up selling fulfill your customers' needs. New products must be really better than the original ones.

2. Integrate Instagram

An average order value from Instagram marketing is around $60.00. Instagram has become a world's largest social media platform after facebook than any other. If you use right filters, appropriate hashtags and post at the right time, then you are on the right path on Instagram.

You can run campaigns, contests and share user generated pictures on Instagram. It is an excellent way to attract users towards your offerings. Instagram is one of the fastest growing apps and can be integrated with your store to have a better user engagement.

3. Launch A Facebook Store

Nobody in their right mind should iagnore Facebook, the biggest platform for social media marketing. What many people are not aware of is that it is also a great source to generate traffic for shopify users since it is well integrated with Shopify store; you don't have to have a separate track of your inventory changes. Facebook Store, an app built by Shopify lets you display and sell your products directly on your Facebook page. Buyers can share their favorite items with their friends.

4. CAPTURE MORE EMAIL SUBSCRIBERS

Email is one of the most essential means at your disposal in eCommerce marketing. It drives online traffic to your store. Email marketing is one of the oldest and still the best channel for digital marketing because it is more direct and accessible. If you are not convinced, consider these stats:

Emails have an ROI of around 4,300%.

80% of people claim that they receive marketing messages with their personal emails regularly.

70% of people make use of discount offers.

So don't ignore the power of good old email. Getting your target customers subscribe to your emails is one of the most surefire ways of increasing sales.

5. IMPROVE EMAIL CAMPAIGNS

It is not sufficient to gather a bunch of email addresses. Sending emails regularly with targeted content and offers is critical. There could be many occasions for sending emails that your subscribers appreciate.

For instance, send a welcome email once the customers sign up. This helps have the highest open rates of any marketing e-mails. Or you can let your customers know that their order is being processed and on its way. They would love to know their order status.

6. Generate More Product Review

As per the online magazine Internet Retailer, one can boost eCommerce conversion rate by 14-76% by adding product reviews to eStores.

There are two key reasons why this is so. First is social proof. Product reviews are similar to testimonials, wherein people share their experiences after using particular products. Second key reason is, SEO. Product reviews help increase the amount of content on web pages and also increases the probability of ranking for long tail keywords.

When you understand all the things about your Instagram strategy, then you can move up to your online business. This is one of the most engaging social communities out there today. To tap into all of its marketing potential, you have to invest a lot of time. But what happens when you find yourself without enough time to spend on your account?

With Instagram, as with any other social media account, if you are not going to be an active participant, then you might as well not sign up.

This visual social network was not created with efficiency in mind, making it one of the most frustrating aspects of a brand's social media marketing strategy. So, how do you make sure that you can include Instagram without all of the frustration that comes with it?

Here are some helpful tips on how to get the most out of the time you spend on the social network without sucking up all of your time.

points To Be Kept In Mind While Instagram Marketing

Use a scheduling app

If you have been on social media long enough, then you know that there is a peak time for posting. It is different for each brand and depends largely on when your audience is the most active.

Do your research and find out when that peak time is for your followers. This makes it most likely to see engagement from your audience when you post.

INSTAGRAM MARKETING STRATEGY

The ideal time to post on Instagram is not always going to be the most convenient for your schedule. For example, how can you make sure that you are posting those images at 5 p.m. every Friday when you have end-of-week meetings set up during that time?

Simple solution: employ a scheduling app. There are plenty of them out there. Find the one you like and line up the posts you want to add throughout the week or month. Schedule the date and time you want each post released. And then go on with your day.

Respond to comments with help

An important part of creating brand loyalty on social media is to take time to reply to your followers' comments. They want to know that their comments are being acknowledged. This can be hard when your following grows and you start to get a lot of comments on your posts each day.

Luckily, you can employ the help of apps to make it easy to reply back.

You can choose from apps like InstaCommentor and Iconosquare to save you time with keeping up with your comments.

Cross-post with one app

When you posting an another post on your related accounts you can also collaborate for your business, that is one of the best marketing strategy that you can use. But how can you do that without having to spend a lot of time on your phone?

Employ the If This, Then That app. IFTTT is a fantastic tool for helping brands cross-post their content without having to go in and manually post.

With this app, you create a sort of "recipe" that will save you time on social media. Basically, you create a formula of what you want to happen when you do something else.

Today's technology, specifically the number of apps that are available, make it so easy to take control of your social media marketing and make it fit into your schedule. This is especially helpful when it comes to the time-consuming aspects of Instagram.

When you use social media to share images that relate to your business, you will forge stronger relationships with your current fans and customers plus broaden your reach to find new ones. Not only are you able to share pictures of your products and therefore the people that exerting to stay your business running (even if it's just you and your pet ferret!), but you'll encourage your customers to submit their own pictures of your products being put to use.

It is easy to lose track of time when you log in to your social media accounts. This is very true with Instagram, where you'll easily lose an hour just scanning through the big variety of images in your stream.

Spending time online is vital for your business, but if it isn't productive time, then it's simply time wasted. Wasted time doesn't help usher in new sales. This is why you would like to possess daily goals for every of your social network activity like once you go online to Instagram.

Before you begin your day, skills much time you would like to allot to social media and every individual network. Stick with that point limit in order that you'll make certain you're getting the foremost important tasks wiped out some time frame and do not allow yourself to urge sucked in to the rabbit burrow that's the web .

Each time you go online to Instagram, confirm you're doing these three things to take care of a high level of efficiency to grow your brand presence:

Add to the number of people you follow

Give yourself about 10-15 minutes every day to start out trying to find Instagram users in your target market. You can do this by looking at who is following your competitors. Find people that are more engaging with the brands they follow since they're more likely to interact with you also . Are they leaving comments and liking photos often?

Share your own content

Take 10 minutes each day to feature new unique content to your own Instagram account. People want to ascertain that you simply have an honest amount of interesting content for them to seem at if they're getting to follow you. If they appear at your stream and only see two pictures and zip new added within the last month or more, they are not getting to see a reason to become a follower.

If you do not have any unique content to share, found out a time every day to easily specialise in taking pictures to share. It are often shots of your products, your office, employees, etc. If it relates to your brand and business, take a stimulating shot of it and edit it to your liking and share.

Be interactive

It's no surprise that once you have a social media account, people expect you to be, well, social. Don't simply check in for an account then await people to start out following you.

To achieve success in your Instagram marketing, you would like to be actively engaging. Reply to comments left on your images, even if it's a simple thank you. Ask questions and encourage a dialog together with your followers.

Visit your followers' streams and people of the folks that you're following and like images and leave comments. Showing that you simply are going to be interactive with other users will go an extended way in building your own brand's following.

Instagram will be around for a long time. To be the foremost effective, you would like to be able to spend time together with your account and be productive thereupon time.

Since social media is all about give and take, confirm that you simply are following an honest number of people and businesses and bloggers. Do your own justifiable share of liking and commenting also .

When looking to usher in more clients, people address social media. While true, tons of website and business owner ditch Instagram as it is a smaller operation in comparison with other sites. However, this is often an error , and a sensible entrepreneur must use Instagram if he or she wants to seek out more clients. With this in mind, there are some drawbacks. Here is some tips given on how to use Instagram for your business.

A picture is valuable: As is often said, a picture is worth a thousand words. Think about it, when running a corporation , one will want to use images to point out off their product or service. This is especially important when selling food, weight loss products or the other items that folks like to check out and luxuriate in . However, one can take it further and boast travel destinations or any number of things. Simply put, this is often one among the simplest tips for using Instagram for business as an image will really show visitors truth value of a product or service.

Younger crowd: Now, when looking to seek out new clients, one will usually want to travel after an older crowd. Yes, while tons of teenagers and young adults use Instagram, not all of them have the cash to spend. However, there are chances to get them hooked and coming back when they are older. Either way, when trying to find the simplest strategy for Instagram, one must remember that not all people can lay out any cash.

Not business-minded: When following their favorite celebrity online, tons of individuals aren't curious about anything but wasting idle time. Meaning, while on Instagram, tons of individuals are simply looking to pass a while on the train and haven't any intention of paying any money.

Your Instagram page may be a thanks to make an excellent first impression on any potential prospects. And the best thanks to make an awesome first impression is take great photos and videos.

Your Instagram page may be a thanks to make an excellent first impression on any potential prospects. And the best thanks to make an awesome first impression is take great photos and videos.

1. Lighting

Bear in mind that no amount of filtering or editing will save a photo that's badly lit. Use natural light whenever you can, except in cases where you have access to the right kind of lighting set-up. If you're taking pictures outside, early morning and late afternoon are the best times.

2. Grab Eye Catching Photo

Before you take out your phone and start snapping pictures, take a moment to really look at what's going on around you. Before you post in Instagram use an eye catching post to structure the photo in your mind. Don't just take out your smart phone and start snapping.

What's in the background of the photo? Is someone close to enter front of your subject? Is there something going on nearby that might mean taking this picture in a different location would be a better idea? Spend a while watching your subject, your surroundings, lighting and everything else that's happening before you begin clicking away.

3. Use Technology

Instagram provides a variety of filters and editing tools. There are also third-party apps which improve the capability of your smart phone camera. There's nothing improper with using apps and tools to take good pictures. Most smart phones have some kind of photo adjusting features and built into their cameras.

They usually include tools that let you cut, switch, modify lighting and contrast levels, increase or decrease saturation, add shadows, shades and highlights and create the long exposure effects.

4. MOVE AROUND YOUR SUBJECT

The lens of smart phone camera soaks up light in a different way in comparison to a traditional camera. When looking through your phone at your subject while moving through a full circle, you'll see how the shifting direction of your light sources can uncover some fantastic effects, and surprising results. You'll start to observe opportunities that previously didn't occur when you just held your phone up and clicked a picture.

5. CHANGE YOUR VIEWPOINT

Shooting from up high or right down on the bottom may result in additional interesting pictures and makes your them look different. Photos that stand out get shared. This is how one photograph on Instagram can go viral, earn you loads or maybe thousands of followers, and assist you draw attention to your business.

INSTAGRAM INFLUENCER MARKETING

Facebook Ads, eBooks, YouTube Marketing, Twitter, and Blogging, they're one among those new marketing methods that appear a day or hebdomadally and truly, they are doing help businesses boost their online confidence and marketing. But, it are often exciting to detect which trendy marketing strategies are real. We know there's one thing that reigns from all those methods: Influencer Marketing, truth! But what is the connection of Influencer Marketing to Instagram Marketing?

If you are not much familiar on what is Influencer Marketing, it is a form of marketing which focuses on utilizing key ambassadors to spread the concept and the message of your brand to their audiences, to your target market, and possibly to a larger market. Instagram has more than 300 million monthly users, and 70% of Instagram users have already searched for brands on the same platform who wanted to guzzle their content. That is why Instagram marketing is effective for your e-commerce business if used right.

Instead of marketing directly to a group of consumers, you may want to hire and inspire influencers to spread the word for you. Well, Instagram has become a place for influencers, a lot of them had grown their audience from small to millions in a short period of time. These internet celebrities have enormous authority over a germinating audience of untouched consumers. They have vast of influence over their audience and may impact latest trends available. If you are working with them? You will be able to speed up the development of your product in a short period of time.

For businesses, you should start identifying the right influencers to work with. This is somewhat the inflexible part of the whole process, you don't want to mess up things at this stage as it affects your whole marketing strategy. Take note, if influencers don't like working with your brand, then stop pleasing them, you don't have to pressure a relationship onto an influencer, if you kept on begging them, chances are they will praise your product in a fake way, ending in a lot of comments saying "spam" from the audience. Once you have found the perfect person for your project, offer to run a trial campaign before pursuing deeper on the relationship.

Using Instagram Analytics tools is important in order to track the important metrics such as comments, engagements, and call-to-action that has great impact to your business.

It is to be noted that you should be involved with your team regarding the strategy for the campaign, in order to get updated on your campaigns. If you accomplish this efficiently, be amazed by the result and benefits that influencer marketing can have on your business.

Instagram Influencers are users with a big audience who are often one among your customers.

Marketing on Instagram grows your website traffic and number of views per month. Yes, Instagram is just that powerful!

Below I give you the top tips for all affiliate marketers. If you're trying to sell your direct sales products using Instagram you would like to stay reading.

#1: Tell People What to try to to

Nothing will grow your business faster than telling your audience what you would like them to try to to . this is often a Call to Action. It works, it's time tested, and it's true. within the fast paced world of social media, you want to show your audience how you'll help them. Then you immediately tell them where to travel for that help. You need to find out that particular thing that your audience needs actually.

From our first-hand experience, Instagram may be a unique social media channel during this respect. A typical person on Instagram will to seem at an image , check the outline , and follow the decision to action. Simple as that. To earn sales on Instagram you would like to provides a call to action "Click the link in profile if you want to find out more!"

From experience, when the decision to action precedes the amazing provide you with get more leads.

Sounds amazing right? Well guess what? It works.

There are some ways to entice your audience. It all begins with putting the proper images and calls to action out there.

#2. Identify Your Audience's Preference

Images that appeal to the customer's preference is that the most vital step for monetizing business on Instagram.

Finding, targeting, and staying relevant to your audience is that the critical factor. And whether you create the foremost income from this platform.

Identifying your audience's preference may be a huge topic. I even have seen what happens when business owners post the incorrect content to the specified audience. Let's just say it is not pretty!

Luckily, you're reading this with some understanding of your audience's preferences. So this could be simple. Take a look back through your Instagram feed and inspect the favored posts. What ahas received comments, shares and likes? Your audience will have an equivalent tastes and preferences you are doing . Tell your audience a brief description and take feedback from them to what to get him and how to use it. If you answer yes, then you've found great content.

Consider getting to your competitor's pages also . inspect their popular posts and pictures . As you discover images your niche audience is interacting with, make similar ones for your page.

Once you've established your audience's preferences, you'll attend subsequent step.

#3 Identify the Profit Locations

Your monetization options on Instagram stay limited once you represent an immediate sales company. Most direct sales companies don't allow their affiliates to require out advertising space. Read the fine print on your affiliate membership. likelihood is that good that paid advertising isn't allowed.

Do you remember tip #1?

But wait. don't post your affiliate link during this location, create an intriguing freebie instead. In business, main goal is to provide satisfaction and get engaged with the potential customer . you'll post this freebie link on Instagram and any social network. This link will collect email leads from folks that want more information.

What is content? Content is information your niche audience wants. If you represent the make-up industry then maybe a freebie on the way to contour may be a good option. Suppose if you are running your diet, exercise and weight lose industry then you need to tell people about what you provide and what is your main purpose of your industry.

The purpose of these profit locations is to need your Instagram audience and switch them into leads. provides a call to action to "Click the Link within the Profile" within the outline . this is often your profit location. Then after your goal is to set up how to get profit margin from your industry and how to manage it.

#4: Educate, Give Variety and Repeat

After you've got led your audience to the profit location you would like to possess an idea of action. Take the leads who wanted your freebie and switch them into a product sale. Use a different testing from your feedback as well as using your service

Start with education.

A lead who wants your freebie may be a "freebie-seeker'. Until you follow up with education about your valuable products they're going to never buy.

Give them information they have and begin building trust.

Give your leads variety.

A fundamental of bridging the lead into a purchase is to possess a multistep follow-up sequence in situ . Create a marketing plan that comes with email marketing, discounts, and valuable "how to" graphics. consider infographics that teach them a replacement technique together with your products. Tell your audience to attemp the live webinar for your new product launcing for your business. this is often the key to moving them through to the sale, what works for a few people won't work for others. you want to have enough variety to capture sales from many various personalities.

Repitition

Humans got to hear an equivalent message a mean of 12 times before it finally kicks in. you'll feel exhausted at repeating your information about your products over and over. Understandable. But you want to realize that your customers didn't hear you the primary time. they need not heard you the second or third or fourth time!

Don't make the error of thinking your one "before and after" image on Instagram goes to urge you a purchase . the aim of Instagram marketing leads the prospect into a sales environment. it's here where you ask them over and once again . If your audience heard the sales talk the primary time, you'd have already had thousands of sales.

Since that's not the case, then likelihood is that , they need not heard your pitch. Take them off of the social media channel with a call to action. Direct them to a 'profit location'. Put in situ a variable marketing campaign and ask them again, and again, and again.

#5 Analysis & Optimization

Finally, analysis & optimization must be an outsized a part of your Instagram strategy. There are two different analysis techniques you would like to know . Quantitative (measurement) and Qualitative (non-measurement).

Quantitative

Here is where you'll measure the engagement with each image / post. Create (or use an analysis app) where you'll calculate the interaction from each post.

Your desired measurement goes to be the amount of clicks to your link in profile.

You will want to live what percentage of these clicks converted to a lead (they gave you an email). Quantitative measurement shows you revenue potential. When each of these leads follows your marketing campaign (tip #4) you've got an honest start line .

Your goal is to form effective Instagram campaigns. therefore the more data you'll increase this analysis, the simpler you will be .

· Day / time of day posted

· Content type - link, photo, video etc.

· Ratio of link clicks to steer captures.

Use this strategy to create an image of which efforts are profitable, and which are a waste of your time .

Qualitative:

Qualitative analysis is watching the aspects of your marketing that's not numbers. Your chemical analysis will cover the aesthetics of your business. Here are some inquiries to start with.

INSTAGRAM MARKETING STRATEGY

· **Am I providing enough information?**
· **Does my freebie link work well for the Instagram platform?**
· **Given all that i do know about marketing, do I encounter as a "spammer"?**
· **Do you provide a quality to your customer who engaged?**

These qualitative measurements should be one among the foremost important considerations. Are you paying enough attention to the service you only "> that you simply offer or are you just trying to form a buck? Believe us. People know the difference between a sales person and someone who leads with value.

The only way you'll make sales is by being the price leader first through qualitative analysis . The more value you divulge the more success you'll experience.

This process may be a long one.

Again, trust us. Take the time to represent yourself because the worth leader and you will earn greater profit within the top of the day .

Here is a some tips for Instagram to promote your business:

1. **Tell people what to try to to**
2. **Identify your audience's preferences**
3. **Identify the profit location**
4. **Educate, variety, and repetition**
5. **Analysis and optimization**

Follow these steps and you'll be head and shoulders above your industry competition. Direct sales is profitable on social media. But you want to prove that you simply are beneficial to your audience first.

Keeping your Instagram busy may be a great way to create your following. a lively account is more interesting than an inactive one. Plus, using Instagram to share all kinds of content together with your audience in many forms goes to be far more interesting to them than if you shared just one type.

Let's check out some ideas that you simply can incorporate into your stories to create your following.

1. Show each day within the Life

A great use of Instagram stories is to require each day and show up a couple of different times of the day to share what you're doing because it relates to your audience and your business. for instance , if you are a business coach, you would possibly want to share how you run your own business and team with others.

INSTAGRAM MARKETING STRATEGY

2. Go Live

Take a while to travel live every day even to share only one exciting tidbit of stories. once you go live randomly, your audience will get notified if they signed up to be notified. They'll pay more attention to you and can even be sad if they miss it live, but they'll also watch the recording if you allow one.

3. Provide a Sneak Peek

Creating a replacement product or service? Provide a sneak peek about it. Trying out a replacement software you would like to recommend? Do a story about it. The more reasons you'll find to point out up in stories, the higher for your quest to seek out more followers.

4. Conduct a Poll

Instagram allows you to conduct polls, which may be a great way to seek out out what your audience is thinking. Keep polls short and sweet to avoid any confusion, since these polls aren't very scientific. If you would like accurate results, consider keeping choices limited.

5. Trade Instagram Stories for each day

If you've got a colleague that serves an identical or same audience as you are doing, you'll trade Instagrams for each day. You run their stories, and that they run yours. this is often an exquisite thanks to get cross-promotion and more followers.

6. count to Launch

If you've got a launch or an occasion arising, use Instagram stories to try to to a countdown for the launch. this is often a fun thanks to get everyone excited about your new offer.

7. Use Stickers and computer graphics

Instagram has ways for you to grab your audience's attention; use them. Add computer graphics, use stickers, add great ahashtags. Call out the proper people. Make yourself known in order that you'll grab those followers who such as you.

When you do share a story, always remember to incorporate a call to action. Your audience won't act (or only very rarely) if you do not tell them what to try to to. whenever you create any content, you ought to know what you would like the results to plan your audience views it.

Marketing On Instagram

Just like the other social network, good results come from increasing your following on a continuing basis. The more people that network together with your posts and brand, the larger your potential audience for every post.

Instagram and Instagram ads provide you with the chance to attach with the people in your niche during a fun, visual way. it is easy to use if you've got a smartphone. Take a photograph , upload it, and your followers will see it and be ready to interact with it.

Provide a Call to Action

Set an objective for every post and use the target to determine your call to action, for instance "register now" or "buy now."

Use The Analytics

The analytics on Instagram allow your business to ascertain how well your various campaigns are working. you've got to convert to a business account to access the tools. The tools will then assist you have an understanding of how your followers are engaging together with your content, so you'll get even better results.

Don't Over-post

Set up the time bound to upload a post then look for result and check when most of your engagement made and come. Then add posts steadily, or reduce your posting if you're getting a smaller amount of engagement.

Instagram Stories

Instagram stories allow businesses to interact with their customers and prospects by making a series of images so as to inform a story.

The important thing to recollect about Instagram stories is they are not everlasting. the pictures and videos remain on your feed for less than 24 hours, then disappear. Instagram stories are often used for increased brand awareness, getting more subscribers and generating sales. Post your stories at a time you recognize is fashionable your users, so as to form the foremost of the 24-hour cycle.

Engage Your Instagram Followers the proper Way

We've been talking lately about how amazing a tool Instagram are often for your business. Instagram is chock filled with marketing opportunities - from paid ads to IGTV to product posts.

However, capturing people's attention is not just about sharing a picture and collecting Likes and followers. you would like to spend time interacting with people and liking other users' posts - time that a lot of business owners simply do not have .

INSTAGRAM MARKETING STRATEGY

Managing a business Instagram account is another task on your to-do list that's already full of meetings, deadlines and projects.

Short on time, an enormous mistake many businesses make is trying to shop for Instagram followers or engagement.

If you're thinking of shopping for Instagram followers or using Instagram bots to undertake and increase engagement, don't.

Here's 2 big reasons why you would like to avoid paying for Instagram followers:

1. Instagram Bots aren't Human

It may seem tempting to shop for Instagram followers and have bots automatically comment, like posts and auto-follow Instagram in your niche. Using Instagram bots makes it appear as if you've got tons of followers and comments - often in hours or days.

For example, an Instagram bot could comment "Awesome!"

The problem with Instagram bots is that they aren't real. They're robots. you are not growing your followers organically with people genuinely curious about your service or product, and you'll ditch engagement.

Many Instagram users are knowing Instagram bots and won't follow someone who leaves a one-word discuss their post. If they begin realizing you're using bots, they could react negatively towards your brand and cause other users to hitch in too.

Use bots they could even jeopardize your account.

Bots also can leave comments that do not add up and may be downright insensitive, like "So cool!" on a tragic post. Bots don't understand the context of the conversation, they simply add comments supported a hashtag.

2. Buying Instagram Followers may be a Big Fake

It are often enticing to strengthen your numbers fast by buying Instagram followers, especially once you see how cheap it's - sites like Buzzoid charge as little as $3 per every 100 followers.

Well, first off: if you purchase Instagram followers you are going against Instagram's Terms of Use.

Instagram monitors fake followers and deletes their accounts so it's likely you'll eventually find yourself losing paid followers and your Instagram account could suffer.

Other issues with buying Instagram followers include:

• It doesn't increase engagement because the bots don't engage together with your content.

- It destroys your brand reputation as your audience sees that you simply have a high number of followers but limited engagement.

There's no easy thanks to grow your Instagram followers. If you're taking shortcuts, you're running the danger of being banned by Instagram and ruining your reputation.

You're more happy posting engaging content, interacting with people, and using the right hashtags to draw in and retain your audience.

It's simple: you cannot automate the extent of human interaction today's Instagram users expect from brands.

Instagram as a social media platform may be a huge buzz. Picture sharing, video sharing, live stories, geolocation, hashtag feed, multiple picture post, improvements within the DM feature, stickers and polls for Instagram stories and an entire new bunch of advanced features for the platform are being added fairly often on the appliance .

Limited only to being a Smartphone application and a clear website, Instagram has emerged out together of the foremost used and loved social apps today.

Having said all this, what's equally talked about is that the Instagram API update and therefore the Instagram API changes. Exasperation spread among brands and marketers everywhere after the discharge of the Instagram API changes.

Before and after the Instagram API access update

Before the discharge of the Instagram API, businesses had to look at metrics via insights on the appliance . But, metrics insights can now be accessed on the new API platform that's equipped during a better way.

Tracking performance of the organic content on third-party tools will now be easier with this API as it's now built on an equivalent approach as is Facebook's Graph API.

The new metrics and insights will empower businesses to remain ahead within the race for the performance of their organic content over what they formerly were receiving with third-party tools.

Why is Instagram metrics and analytics required for tracking a customer behavior?

Instagram analytics may be a crucial a part of Instagram marketing strategies. Marketing efforts put in by brands can amount to being a waste of cash and resources without appropriate analytics reports. Analytics help in determining how great are the marketing strategies. What results are obtained after applying the marketing strategy etc. are often tracked easily for improving the performance and approach towards marketing and advertising content.

Brand performance on Instagram are often easily decoded with Instagram analytics with the new Instagram API update.

Content monitoring feature

Instagram API update is inclusive of a replacement functionality that permits businesses to limit and moderate content. Businesses can efficiently use this feature to cover comments in light of organic content. As a versatile choice to display or to not display comments and toggle between them, this ensures a healthy platform is maintained for expression of thoughts.

In addition to the present feature, an automatic system also detects offensive and provoking comments and helps businesses in their content moderation practices.

Business profile compatibility with the Instagram API update

Instagram is ideal for you to grow your business:

1. Instagram is Instantaneous

There is no waiting around until you revisit to your home or office to require full advantage of Instagram for brand building.

2. No Duplicate Accounts Needed

Unlike Facebook and Google+ where you're required to line up a lengthy personal profile before you'll found out a brand page, you're allowed to leap right in as a brand on Instagram with none consequence. it is a fairly easy found out process. It will make your account restrict from Instagram and take legal action in terms of service

3. Everyone Has an Inner-Photographer

Many business owners are at a loss when it involves using social networks to grow their customer base for the foremost part because they are doing not have how with words or skills to hone their creative juices for content marketing. But everyone likes taking photos and let's be honest - almost all folks seems like we've a knack behind the camera.

4. It Makes Your Brand Look Interesting

This is the good thing about using Instagram to showcase your product/service. Use Instagram to point out off your product/service and even your corporate culture by capturing candid office moments. Instagram albums give personality to brands during a manner that no other sharing network has been ready to accomplish so far.

5. Create a Location Page for Your Business

Google Places and therefore the new Google+ Local Pages for businesses have proven the importance of getting a physical location attached to your brand's online presence. Instagram's integration with the Foursquare location database allows you to Geotag the situation the photo was taken from (i.e. your home of business) which allows it to be added to the situation page on Instagram. It is also good to use google my business to help people who find your business in anyway in nearest area. If users are browsing photos supported location and see a product of yours that appeals to them within their area, you'll have a replacement customer. If a location isn't listed, you'll add your business to the Instagram/Foursquare database.

6. It's Easier to urge Followers

Because you cannot post links on Instagram, the general public won't desire they're being bombarded with SPAM when following your brand account. If you regularly post interesting images that feature your product service on Instagram, customers are more likely to follow you there than on the other Social Network. it'll be easier for you to create brand recognition with a much bigger fan base. Because Instagram easily links to your Facebook and Twitter accounts, it helps those social networks grow for you also . an equivalent rules of social network marketing apply though - interact with (comment and "like") and follow your customers FIRST. On Instagram, they really follow back.

6 Golden guiding principles

1. Use a business account

In case you skipped the previous section with the intention of following the tips below while using a personal account, here's why it's best to reconsider your decision.

Personal account holders cannot access certain features of the business account, such as :

Instagram Insights, Instagram advertisements, Instagram's Shopping feature, Contact information and the call to action button on your profile.

The Creator account provides special benefits for influencers and content creators. The Business account remains the most suitable solution for marketers

2. Clearly define your objectives

All social platforms are tools that you can't use effectively unless you have well defined your goals.

Instagram marketing: it can take on different aspects depending on the marketers. You are looking for :

Develop your brand awareness?

Obtain new leads?

Establish your brand as an industry leader?

Stimulate your sales?

You may well combine several elements, but it is imperative to know the purpose of your Instagram strategy in order to achieve the desired results. We've published a comprehensive blog article on how to define your goals so you can determine your priorities.

3. Define your audience

A little preliminary research can help you determine who you might be interested in on Instagram. For example, our article on Instagram demographics reveals that :

The most active instagrammers are between the ages of 18 and 29.
The United States is the largest market for Instagram.
Instagram is more popular in the city than in the suburbs.
But don't just use Instagram to reach only Americans in cities in their 20s. Instead, you need to define your target market in order to create content that speaks directly to that audience.
This point will also play a crucial role in the targeting choices for your Instagram ads.

4. Optimize your profile

In just 150 characters, your bio Instagram should make a good first impression, convey your brand identity and tell users why it's important to track your Instagram account.
That's a lot to ask for so little text.
Fortunately, your Instagram profile has additional fields to showcase your brand and help people find you. These are :
Your name: 30 characters, included in the search.
Your username: Your nickname. Up to 30 characters, included in the search.
Your website: the clickable URL that you can change as often as you like.
Your category: a professional feature that tells users your type of activity, saving you space in your bio.
Your contact information: which indicates where you can be found.
Call to action buttons: to allow instagrammers to interact with you directly from your profile page.

5. Choose a good profile picture

Most brands use their logo as an Instagram profile picture. This contributes to their credibility and allows visitors to identify them instantly.

The Instagram profile picture is in the form of a circle 110 pixels in diameter. However, since it is stored at a resolution of 320 by 320 pixels, it is recommended that a file of this size be uploaded to ensure a good rendering should Instagram change its display.

If your logo is square, you will need to zoom out to make sure it appears completely within the circle.

6. Publish at the right time

MDid you know that the best time to post on Instagram varies depending on your industry?

We've analyzed nearly 259,000 publications from 11 different sectors and found that there is an ideal publication time for each, even though the Instagram feed is no longer chronological.

Here are the results of our study:

- Travel and Tourism: Fridays between 9:00 a.m. and 1:00 p.m.
- Media and Entertainment: Tuesday and Thursday, 12:00 to 3:00 p.m.
- Catering: Friday at noon
- Retail: Tuesday, Thursday and Friday at noon
- Professional Services: Tuesday, Wednesday and Friday at 9:00 or 10:00 a.m.
- Non-profit organizations: Tuesdays, 10 a.m. or 4 p.m.
- E-commerce other than retail: Thursdays at 4:00 p.m. or 9:00 p.m.
- Pharmacy and health: Wednesday and Sunday at 9 a.m.
- Personal care: Thursday and Friday at 1, 2 or 3 p.m.
- Technology: Monday and Tuesday at 2 p.m.
- Education: Thursdays at 4 or 5 p.m.

www.ingramcontent.com/pod-product-compliance
Lightning Source LLC
Chambersburg PA
CBHW041946240526
45473CB00033B/619